PRACTICAL ATHEISM

IN

DENYING THE AGENCY OF PROVIDENCE

DETECTED AND EXPOSED.

BY

REV. JAMES NALL.

"The lot is cast into the lap, but the whole disposing thereof is of the Lord."—Prov., 16:33.

"The eyes of the Lord run to and fro throughout the whole earth, to show Himself strong in behalf of them whose heart is perfect towards Him."—2 Chron., 16:9.

DETROIT, MICH.:
PRINTED BY WM. H. THOMPSON & CO., 208 JEFFERSON AVENUE.
1873.

TO

The Believers

IN

A Superintending Providence

THIS LITTLE BOOK

IS

Respectfully Dedicated

BY THE AUTHOR.

PREFACE.

Among the many important subjects which from time to time engage our attention, there is not one so ripe with solid and abiding satisfaction as the superintendence of an all-wise and gracious Providence in the management of human affairs.

Accident, chance, fortune, and a violation of the laws of nature, are terms often heard, and much in the life of man is ascribed to them. If the blessings of prosperity fall to their lot, they take the credit and the honor to themselves, and ascribe it to their own skill and industry, to their own economy and prudence. If riches take to themselves wings and fly away, some one else must bear the blame. If calamities overtake them, they are ascribed to some unlucky accident. If affliction seizes their bodies, and death enters their families, it is owing to a violation of some of the laws of nature.

But such a belief is repugnant to reason, dishonorable to God, and is practical atheism.

It is contrary to reason to suppose that God, who formed the heavens and created the universe, who has beautified it with so many ornaments, and peopled it with so many rational beings, should abandon it to blind chance, or leave it without His superintendence and government.

No; He who appoints the sun, moon and stars their course, and gives laws and boundaries to the great deep that it cannot pass, is not, cannot be, unmindful of man, the master-piece of creation, and the Church which He has purchased by the precious blood of His dear Son.

To establish this fact is the object of the following pages, and the importance of the subject is the author's plea in giving them to the public.

CONTENTS:

CHAP. XI.

CHAP. XII.

CHAP. XIII.

CHAP. XVI.

PRACTICAL ATHEISM

IN

Denying the Agency of Providence

DETECTED AND EXPOSED.

CHAPTER I.

The doctrine of a Superintending Providence is taught in various forms in almost every part of the Bible.

The reality of a Superintending Providence is so clearly revealed in the Scriptures of Truth as effectually to remove every doubt from the minds of those who attentively read and believe them.

To decide matters of doubt or difficulty by the casting of lots was a common practice among the ancients and the primitive saints. When an Apostle was to be chosen to fill the place of Judas, the vacancy was supplied by the casting of lots. To find out who was the guilty person with whom God was angry, the troubled mariners cast lots, and the lot fell upon Jonah. The Promised Land was divided among the Jews by the casting of lots. The selection of the scape goat was determined by the casting of lots. And the orders and services of the priests were assigned them by the casting of lots.

It is not easy to determine as to the manner of casting lots, because we have no certain information upon the subject. But from a passage in the Book of Proverbs, where it is said: "The lot is cast into the lap, but the whole disposing thereof is of the

Lord," would lead us to suppose that the instruments employed on such occasions were cast into the lap, or on the fold of a garment, and drawn after a perfect mingling of them together.

But in all their decisions by the casting of lots, they never failed to recognize the hand of God. What they did was always with the strictest reference to Him who is the wise disposer of all events, with whom is left the decision and the judgment.

The supreme dominion of Providence over the affairs of kingdoms and nations is repeatedly and strongly asserted. "The Lord hath prepared His throne in the heavens, and His kingdom ruleth over all." "He doeth according to His will in the armies of heaven and among the inhabitants of the earth." "Behold, He taketh away, and who shall hinder Him? and who shall say unto Him, 'What doest thou?'"

The promotion and abasement of princes are ascribed to Divine agency. "Promotion cometh neither from the east nor the west, nor from the south; but God is the Judge. He putteth down one and setteth up another." "He changeth the times and the seasons. He removeth kings and setteth up kings." "The Most High ruleth in the kingdom of men, and giveth it to whomsoever He will." And sometimes, for the accomplishment of His designs, He gives it to an usurper and a tyrant.

Sickness and health, peace and war, na-

tional blessings and calamities, are represented as being at the disposal of an all-wise and gracious Providence. "Is there evil in a city and the Lord hath not done it? "Come, behold the works of the Lord; what desolations He hath made in the earth. He maketh war to cease unto the ends of the earth; He breaketh the bow and cutteth the spear in sunder; he burneth the chariot in the fire."

The watchful care of Providence is said to extend *to all the lower works of creation.* He giveth the beast his food, and feedeth the young ravens when they cry. "Behold the fowls of the air, they sow not, neither do they reap nor gather into barns, yet your Heavenly Father feedeth them." "H clothes the grass of the field, which to-day is and to-morrow is cast into the oven." And again it is said, " The hairs of your head are all numbered."

And shall the Divine Being exercise a kind, watchful care over lillies and the grass of the field, over ravens and sparrows, and even over the hairs of our heads, and shall He not kindly watch over *the children of men and the nations of the earth?* Shall He watch over *sparrows* and overlook *man*, who is of more value than many sparrows? Shall He keep a watchful care over the hairs of a *man's* head, and shall he overlook *man himself?* No; the idea is absurd, and is opposed to reason, as well as unscriptural. There is either a kind, watchful Providence continually presiding over the children of men, or the Bible is not true; for there nothing is more plainly taught and more repeatedly and strongly asserted.

CHAPTER II.

The agency of Providence in the management of human affairs is, and ever has been, a prominent doctrine in the creeds of all evangelical Christians.

Firmly believing in the Divine supremacy, all evangelical Christians look to Him for support in the day of trouble, for protection in the time of danger, for guidance in the hour of perplexity, for assistance to supply every necessity, and for wisdom to devise, and zeal to execute, every plan of usefulness.

It is on this account that Christians meet and sing:

> "Except the Lord conduct the plan,
> The best concerted schemes are vain
> And never can succeed."

If our bodily afflictions, our painful bereavements, and our various earthly calamities, come upon us by chance, or accident, or by a violation of the laws of nature, then to pray to God for His interposition would be an incongruity, an empty compliment, a solemn mockery. For if He exerts no agency in such cases, where is the propriety or consistency of imploring His favor? If He leaves all things to their natural course, "then we have nothing to fear from His displeasure on account of sin, and we have nothing to expect from His assistance, and consequently it is needless and absurd to humble ourselves for the one, or to be importunate for the other."

But such is not, and never has been, the doctrine of evangelical Christians. They regard the Supreme Being as the great and wise governor of the world, who is too wise ever to err, and too good ever to be unkind.

Their bodily afflictions, their distressing bereavements, their domestic trials, their losses in business, come not out of the dust, spring not out of the ground, they fall not by chance, they are not unlucky accidents, they are not occasioned by the violation of a natural law. No; they are all the appointments of a father and a friend. And this is an assurance which cannot fail to tranquilize the heart of the Christian, and give it confidence. It is this delightful assurance that leads the sufferer to forget his anguish, that wipes away the orphan's tear, turns into a smile the widow's sigh, and with the bitter draught of misery mingles the wine of consolation. This reconciles the Christian to his lot, and leads him to bow submissively, and say with the pious Psalmist: "I was dumb; I opened not my mouth, because Thou didst it"

CHAPTER III.

To the universal agency of Providence we have the recorded testimony of those who were shut up in all the darkness of heathenism.

Hear the testimony of Nebuchadnezzar, the Chaldean monarch: "And at the end of the days, I, Nebuchadnezzar, lifted up mine eyes unto heaven, and mine understanding returned unto me, and I blessed the Most High, and I praised and honored Him that liveth forever, whose dominion is an everlasting dominion, and His kingdom is from generation to generation. And all the inhabitants of the earth are reputed as nothing: and He doeth according to His will in the army of heaven, and among the inhabitants of the earth; and none can stay His hand, or say unto Him: 'What doest thou.'"

Listen again to the testimony of Cyrus, the Persian King: "Thus saith Cyrus, King of Persia: 'The Lord God of Heaven hath given me all the kingdoms of the earth.'" From this language it is quite evident that he regarded all his earthly possessions and his extensive dominion as the gift of a kind, watchful Providence.

The Babylonian General Nebuzaradan

thus addressed the Prophet Jeremiah: "And the Captain of the Guard took Jeremiah and said unto him: 'The Lord thy God hath pronounced this evil upon this place. Now the Lord hath brought it, and done according as he hath said. And now, behold, I loose thee this day from the chains which were upon thy hand.'"

Cicero, the Roman orator, thus acknowledges the universal agency of Providence. After detecting and suppressing the conspiracy of Cataline, instead of taking the glory to himself, he gives it to God: "If I should say it was I that defeated the conspirators, I should take too much upon me, and my arrogance would be insufferable. It was the Supreme God; it was He, it was He that defeated them; it was His will to preserve our capital—His will to preserve this city and these temples, His will that you should all be safe. It was under the conduct of the Immortal God that I formed this judgment and determination, and made such a discovery of the plot."

Thus men who had nothing but the light of nature and tradition for their guide, did not ascribe their defeats and victories, their blessings and calamities, to chance or accident, or the workings of natural laws, but to the doings of the Great Sovereign of the universe. They were then, in this respect, far in advance of those who in our day make their boast of progress. For it is, if I may be allowed to make such a statement, *a progress backward.* They are not only retrograding from the venerable truths of Christianity, but are fast hastening into the lowest depths of infidelity.

CHAPTER IV.

God has a right, and possesses a fitness to be the supreme governor of the world.

God has an unquestionable *right* to govern the world. As He is the creator of all, He has a right to sovereign rule and dominion over all. As He gave all their being, He has a right to appoint all their stations, and to prescribe for their government.

Every man has a limited, and a derived, right over his family. It is derived from his relation as father, and it is limited by the command of God. The world is God's family, over which he has an unlimited and an underived right to preside and govern.

God has not only a right but is *admirably fitted* to govern the world.

His unlimited power gives Him this qualification.

As none but an Omnipotent power could create the world, so none but an Omnipotent power can preserve and govern it. "But all power belongeth unto Him, both in heaven and on earth." Whatever His goodness dictates, and His wisdom plans, His power can always accomplish.

His perfect righteousness gives Him this qualification. If he who hates right is unfit to govern, then He who is infinitely righteous, and who has an infinite love for righteousness, must be admirably fitted to govern the world. He is "glorious in holiness." "Just and right is He."

His infinite wisdom also gives Him this qualification. The wisdom of men, even the wisest of them, is finite and limited. After their most laborious researches, how soon have they said all that they know about the most important and interesting subjects. But the wisdom of God is infinite; His knowledge is boundless. He not only knows all things, but He knows all things perfectly. With Him there is no doubt, no perplexity, no contingency. All that is past, all that is present, and all that is to come, lies open and naked in His sight. How admirably qualified, then, is He to guide the helm of government.

His universal presence gives Him an additional qualification. He is present in every place, and at every instant. There is no place in which He can be included, nor is there any from which He can be excluded. God Himself asks the question: "Do I not fill heaven and earth?" With what sublimity is the Divine Omnipresence taught by the royal Psalmist: "Whither shall I go from Thy spirit? or whither shall I flee from Thy presence? If I ascend up into heaven, Thou art there. If I make my bed in hell, behold, Thou art there. If I take the wings of the morning and dwell in the uttermost parts of the sea, even there shall Thy hand lead me, and Thy right hand shall hold me. If I say,

'Surely, the darkness shall cover me,' even the night shall be light about me. Yea, the darkness hideth not from Thee; but the night shineth as the day; the darkness and the light are both alike to Thee."

This shows with what clearness and accuracy the last judgement will be conducted. The Judge will then decide, not according to what He has thought, or what He has infered, concerning the merit or demerit of men, but according to what He has seen and known of them himself. Then no powerful advocate can be of any service to the wicked, and no false witness can damage the character of the righteous, for God himself was present when the matters brought before Him for decision were perpetrated. Who, then, can doubt His qualification to govern the world, whose presence pervades the universe.

His boundless goodness adds to His fitness to be the supreme governor of the world. The Lord is good in and of Himself, essential, perfect, eternal goodness. His goodness is communicated and extends to every creature. "Thou art good, and Thou doest good," is the language of the pious David. There is not an insect that crawls on the earth, or that flutters in the sunbeam; there is not a fish that swims in the sea, nor a bird that flies in the air, nor a beast that wanders in the desert, nor a creature in the universe below His notice and kind regard; all are the objects of His care and the recipients of His goodness. This is not only a qualification to govern, but an especial source of joy and gladness to the governed.

His long forbearance is another indisputable qualification. Infinite patience, as well as infinite knowledge, must be requisite for such an undertaking. The most perfect of created beings could not behold the disorder, the depravity, and the injustice by which we are surrounded, and the insults which are daily offered to God without being ready to call down fire from heaven to consume such guilty men. But "God suffereth long and is kind." But though He bears long, He will not always bear; He will finally render to every man the just desert of his deeds.

His immutability completes His fitness to rule and govern the world. A character of stability attaches itself to nothing which we now inherit; everything earthly is mutable and given to changes. But God is immutable and unchangeable. "The same yesterday, to-day and forever." What He once knows can never be forgotten, can never be obliterated from His memory. To say that God cannot see is to deprive Him of His Omnipresence. To say that He cannot know is to deprive Him of His Omniscience, and to say that He can ever forget what He once knows is to rob Him of His immutability, and to make Him mutable and changeable like unto ourselves. But He changeth not. In the Epistle to the Hebrews we read: "And Thou, Lord, in the beginning, hath laid the foundation of the earth; and the heavens are the works of Thy hands. They shall perish, but Thou remainest: and they shall wax old, as doth a garment, and as a vesture shalt Thou fold them up, and they shall be changed; but Thou art the same, and Thy years shall not fail." God, then, is not only qualified to be the supreme governor of the world, but His qualifications can never be taken away.

CHAPTER V.

There can be no reason assigned why God should not govern the world, seeing that He has a right and a fitness for it.

If God does not govern the world, it must be either because He *cannot* or *will not* do it. It is not because He *cannot*, for He is Omnipotent; His power is unlimited, and consequently there is nothing which it cannot accomplish. In the beginning, He commanded light to shine out of darkness. "He spake and it was done; He commanded and it stood fast; He said: 'Let there be light,' and there was light." If, then, God does not govern the world, it cannot proceed from His inability, "for all power belongeth unto Him." Inability must proceed either from a want of knowledge, or from a want of power. The one, if asserted, would deny his Omniscience, and make Him an ignorant being; and the other would deny his Omnipotence, and make Him weak and helpless, and consequently no God at all. But His wisdom is infinite and His power is unlimited.

Neither can it be because He *will not* that we are deprived of Divine government. To create such a multiplicity of creatures and rational beings, and neither to care for them nor to provide for them, would be an impeachment of His goodness. But His mercy is infinite, and His goodness is unspeakable. His right and fitness, therefore, to govern is indisputable. His claim cannot be denied without being guilty of practical atheism.

CHAPTER VI.

Divine Providence is universal in its extent, including all beings and all creatures, from the highest to the lowest.

In the Bible much is ascribed to God, but nothing to chance, to accident, to fate, or natural law.

Christ, while upon earth, was under the Divine government. He is, therefore, said to be the gift of God, the sent of God, and the annointed of the Father. All the circumstances connected with His manifestation;

all that Moses in the law and the prophets wrote, and the convulsions and revolutions of nations, were all the arrangements of Him who knows the end from the beginning, to prepare the way for His annointed. Peter denied his Master; Judas betrayed Him; Pilate condemned Him, and the Roman soldiers put Him to death. But these were only the sinful executions of the Divine decree. A bitter cup was presented to Him, but He took it, saying: "The cup which my Father hath given me, shall I not drink it?" "Lo, I came to do Thy will, O, God."

Angels form a part of His family, and are under His government. They are employed as His agents, and are instruments of His providence. They fly to do His bidding.

We have many striking instances of their doings recorded in the Scriptures. The angel Gabriel fled with joyful haste to Daniel to deliver him the Divine message. An angel pursued Hagar into the wilderness and told her to return to her mistress. Three angels appear to Abraham and assure him of the birth of Isaac. Jacob went out on his way, "and the angels met him." An angel delivered Lot from Sodam. An angel led Peter out of prison. And angels were the Savior's principal attendants in all cases of extremity and necessity. An angel was the first publisher of His birth. An angel forewarned His reputed father to provide for His safety. Angels sang over the plains of Bethlehem, "Glory to God in the highest; on earth, peace and good will toward men."

An angel administered succor to His languishing nature in the wilderness. An angel refreshed Him in His agony and bloody sweat. An angel rolled away the stone from the door of the sepulchre. Angels attended His ascension to heaven. And when He shall come a second time to judge the world in righteousness, mighty angels will form His retinue.

His government extends to *evil angels.* He prescribes to them their bounds, and they cannot go one step beyond without His permission. Evil spirit could not enter into the Gadareme swine without leave ; nor could they touch either the person or property of Job without permission.

Man, the masterpiece of creation, is in a

more especial manner the object of Divine care and government. God may sometimes lead him about, crossing his intentions, darkening his prospects, and disappointing his hopes; yet He always leads him in a right way. "The Judge of all the earth shall do right."

His providential care extends to the *elements* and to the *lowest of His creatures*. He tells the thunder when to speak, the lightning when and where to strike, the rain when and where to fall, and to the foaming ocean He says: "Hitherto shalt thou go, but no farther, and here shall thy proud waves be stayed."

The beasts that wander in the forest, the birds that roam in the air, the insects that crawl on the earth, and all the creatures of the sea wait on Him and receive their food at His hand.

The grass on the mountain top, the flowers of the field, and the fruits of the earth, are all the production of His hand, proclaim His goodness and manifest His glory.

I know that some have asserted that it is derogatory to the dignity of God to stoop so low as to concern himself about such insignificant creatures. In reply to this objection, I wish to say that if it was no dishonor for Him to make them, it can be no dishonor for Him to watch over and care for them.

CHAPTER VII.

God's providential dealings are sometimes very mysterious.

He is a God that hideth Himself. He wraps Himself in a cloud, and His way is in the sea. His ways are a height which we cannot reach; they are a depth which we cannot possibly fathom. "He dwelleth in the light which no man can approach unto." How strikingly appropriate, then, is the question which Eliphas addressed to Job: "Can'st *thou*, by searching, find out God;

can'st thou find out the Almighty to perfection?" But though clouds and darkness be round about His throne, "judgment and justice are the habitation thereof forever."

This mystery appears in overruling the wicked designs of men, and bringing good out of the apparent, or intended, evil. Joseph's brethren sold him out of envy, but God overruled it for their good. The Babel builders began to erect a tower to prevent their dispersion; but God made it the very means of their dispersion. Cyrus, out of pride and ambition, went out against Babylon, and took it; but God made it the means, or overruled it, for the deliverance of His people from their seventy years' captivity.

The mysteries of Providence appear *in making the weakest instruments the means of accomplishing, or bringing to pass, the greatest events.* He caused the rod in the hand of Moses to confound the skill of the Egyptian magicians. David, a mere stripling, with a sling and stone is a match for the gigantic champion of the Philistines. The cackling of geese is made the salvation of the Roman capital. And, under the Gospel, God calls the weak things to confound the mighty, and foolish things to confound the wise.

His mysterious purposes are sometimes accomplished *by deeply impressing the mind of one man for the preservation of others.* Mordecai, the Jew, by a mysterious move in the wheel of Providence, is made the favorite of Ahasuerus. The eyes of the King are kept awake—he cannot sleep, and he is induced to pass the night in reading a book, but he could fix upon no book but the records of the kingdom, and no place in those records could engage his attention but the chronicle of Mordecai discovering a treason against the life of the King, which proved the means of his promotion and the deliverance of the Jews from the destructive plot laid by Haman.

At other times His mysterious purposes are brought to pass by *confounding the counsels of men, and turning the wisdom of the wise into foolishness.* We have a remarkable instance of this kind in the case of

Herod. When the wise men of the East came in search of the child Jesus, the King sought a private interview with the wise men, on their arrival, and told them to go to Bethlehem and search diligently for the young child till they found him, and then return to him that he might know where to go to worship Him, though his real design was to take away His life. But God appeared to the wise men in a dream, and told them not to return to Herod, but depart to their own country another way. The angel also appeared to Joseph and told him to take the young child and His mother and flee into Egypt, because Herod would seek Him to destroy Him.

The Jews crucified Christ for fear of losing the favor of Cæsar, and of exposing their country to the prey of the Roman army, which brought upon them the very thing they intended to prevent.

Even those dispensations of providence which are now so dark and afflictive, and which to us, for a time, will remain inexplicable, yet the day will come that will remove every cloud which now vails the wise administrations of His throne. Then shall we be led to adore the wisdom of His government, and join in one universal response: "O, Lord, Thou hast done all things well; just and true are Thy ways, O, Thou King of saints."

CHAPTER VIII.

The dispensations of Providence are sometimes surrounded by darkness.

The dispensations of Providence are not only mysterious, and crooked as the paths of the desert, but dark as the hour of midnight. "He holdeth back the face of His throne, and spreadeth His cloud upon it."

There is the darkness of *His providential dispensations.* If we are blessed with wealth, it is suddenly and unexpectedly taken away. By means of a vessel sinking, a debtor breaking, a devouring fire, or by some unforeseen accident, we are reduced to a condition of poverty and want. If we are blessed with domestic comforts these are taken away. An affectionate wife is severely afflicted, a valuable father is called off the stage of life, a promising son turns out a prodigal, or a beloved Isaac is consigned to the grave. If we possess a character which we value as we do our life, it is assailed by the forked tongue of calumny and the pernicious breath of slander. Or, if we are blessed with bodily health, this is taken away. The fever begins to burn in the frame, or consumption begins to prey upon the vitals and we are laid on a bed of sickness and pain.

An only son, the sole support of hoary-headed widowhood is carried to the grave. A valuable father is taken away from the head of a numerous and dependent family. A kind mother is taken away from her helpless and fatherless children. And who takes them away? Who is the intermeddler in our affairs? "Behold, He taketh away. And who shall hinder Him? or who shall say unto Him, 'What doest Thou?'"

There is the darkness of *spiritual trials.* The soul of the Christian is sometimes enveloped in darkness. He has lost the light of Jehovah's countenance, and he knows not what to do. He fears that the Lord has forgotten and forsaken him. He is about to give up all for lost, to let go the anchor of his hope, and to abandon his little boat to the mercy of the billows. And it is well for the Christian to be sometimes down in the valley, and to be overshadowed with a cloud. If he was always on the mountain top, and always under the cheering rays of spiritual prosperity, he would be in danger of relaxing in his Christian course, and of wandering on the quicksands of pride. These spiritual trials, then, enter into the arrangements of Providence, and are conducting us by an unseen hand to the most desirable ends.

Christian reader, were you ever in a state of spiritual darkness? Did you ever sail in gloominess on the stormy ocean of life? With what loveliness, then, did the shining of the Saviour's face appear when it beamed forth upon you, and comforted your troubled heart.

And what does God design by these spiritual trials? To let us see more of the deformity and the hatefulness of sin, the emptiness and vanity of the world, the excellency of religion and the loveliness of the Saviour.

Let the Christian here learn never to despair. However dark may be his spiritual state, and however boisterous may be his passage, Christ is in the boat and at the helm. The cloud may be dark and dense, but the sun behind never sets. "Let him, then, trust in the Lord, and stay his mind upon his God." In the pelting of the most pitiless storm, let him flee for shelter to the throne of God, and take Him for his strong habitation.

There is the *darkness of death.* And

dense, indeed, is this darkness to the impenitent, ungodly man. He looks back with remorse on a life spent in the dark ways of sin. He looks around but can discover no cheering ray. He looks inward and all is perplexity, his conscience troubles him, and he has a foretaste of that fire which shall never be quenched. He looks upward, but instead of a cheering prospect, the heavens gather blackness over his head; "There remaineth nothing for him but a fearful looking for of judgement and fiery indignation, which shall devour him as an adversary."

The noted infidel who, in the prospect of death, said he was going to take a leap in the dark, in one sense told the truth, for the darkness of sin leads to the darkness of death, the darkness of death to the darkness of judgment, and the darkness of judgment to the blackness of darkness forever.

There is a sense in which death is a dark day to the Christian. To close his eyes upon all visible objects, to tear his heart from those he values and esteems; to feel the pangs of departing life, and to enter upon a state which is unknown and untried, can never be contemplated as a trifle. No; it is a serious thing, even for a Christian, to die. But this only concerns the body. He has nothing to fear on account of the soul. No frightful spectres of unforgiven crimes terrify his thoughts; no uneasy apprehensions of the future depress his joy; no gloomy clouds arise to darken his prospects of future glory. No; "Mark the perfect man, and behold the upright, for the end of that man is peace." "I heard a voice from heaven saying unto me: 'write blessed are the dead who die in the Lord from henceforth. Yea,' saith the spirit, 'for they rest from their labors, and their works do follow them.'"

The dying Christian has before him the cheering prospect of future glory. He is going to put off the helmet and to put on the crown; to lay aside the garments in which he sustained the conflict and to be clothed in white robes; to hang up the weapons of his warfare, to take them down no more forever; to emerge from the darkness of death and to shine forth not only as the stars, having turned many to righteousness, but as the sun in the kingdom of his Father.

The Christian, when dying, is not allowed to pass through the dark valley alone; a kind Providence watches over him there. "Though I walk through the valley and shadow of death I will fear no evil, for Thou art with me; Thy rod and thy staff they comfort me."

To the Christian *light springs up in the midst of darkness*, "To the upright there ariseth light in the darkness." "Sorrow may endure for a night, but joy cometh in the morning."

Go into that comfortless garret, or enter that damp, cold cellar, and if you find a Christian there he will tell you that "godliness with contentment is great gain." He is more thankful for a dinner of herbs than his pampered lord is for all the luxuries of nature. And he is far happier in his miserable abode than an ungodly prince in his magnificent palace.

Hear what is said by the child of God when robbed of his prosperity and left to stand upon the ruins of his worldly hopes: "Shall I receive good at the hand of the Lord, and shall I not receive evil?" "Though Thou slay me, yet will I put my trust in Thee."

Look at that martyred saint. He mounts the scaffold, embraces the stake, and, as he expires in the midst of the flames, he says, with David: "The Lord is my light and my salvation; whom shall I fear? The

Lord is the strength of my life; of whom shall I be afraid?"

Listen to the language of the new-made widow as she gazes upon her orphan children. Conscious that religion gives to the widowed mother a husband more tender and kind than the one consigned to the grave; and to her dear, helpless children a Father full of sympathy and love, she bows to the Disposer of all events, and she says: "Not my will, but Thine, be done." "The Lord gave and the Lord taketh away; blessed be the name of the Lord."

Visit that chamber of sickness and look at that afflicted saint. What hear you there? The gloomy murmurings of discontent? or the heavy groans of despair? No; the voice of joy and gladness is heard in the tabernacles of the righteous. Under the afflictions of his body his spirit is refreshed by a stream that never dries, "but springs up unto everlasting life."

Is the Christian about to die? Death is deprived of its sting; the grave is robbed of all its gloomy terrors. He looks by an eye of faith to the star of Bethlehem, and he is cheered and comforted.

Is the Christian in a state of spiritual darkness, and ready to give up all for lost? Suddenly a beam of mercy breaks through the darkening cloud and cheers him with its reviving rays; and he is enabled once more to steer his course under the unsullied sunbeams of the sun of righteousness.

And who is He who causes such heavenly light to spring up amid surrounding gloom? He who superintends the destinies of men; and who has said: "I am with thee." "I will never leave thee, nor forsake thee."

CHAPTER IX.

We can trace the hand of Providence in the punishment of the wicked; and sometimes in the same manner and to the same extent as they have punished others.

Pharaoh enslaved the people of Israel, multiplied their burdens, and refused to let them go. For this he was visited with numerous and fearful plagues, which ended in the midnight destruction of the first-born of Egypt, and his own final overthrow in the Red sea.

Nebuchadnezzar, the proud King of Babylon, walked about his palace, looked at the gigantic walls and the numerous and magnificent buildings of the city, and then gave expression to his feelings: "Is not this great Babylon that I have built by the might of my power, and for the honor of my majesty?" "While the word was in the King's mouth there fell a voice from heaven, saying: 'O, King Nebuchadnezzar, to thee it is spoken: the kingdom is departed from thee, and they shall drive thee from men, and thy dwelling shall be with the beasts of the field. They shall make thee eat grass as oxen; and seven times shall pass over thee, until thou know that the Most High ruleth in the kingdom of men, and giveth it to whomsoever He will.' The same hour was the thing fulfilled upon Nebuchadnezzar; and he was drivèn from men, and did eat grass as oxen, and his body was wet with the dew of heaven, till his hairs were grown like eagles' feathers, and his nails like birds' claws."

Belshazzar, surrounded by his wives, concubines and nobles, and drinking out of the consecrated vessels of the temple to his vain gods of silver and gold, saw his destiny written upon the plaster of the wall: "*Mene, mene, tekel, upharsin,*" and the very same night fell by the hand of his enemy."

Sannacherib, the Assyrian monarch, came down with his powerful army to sack and destroy the people and cities of Judah; and threatened Jerusalem with a total and an immediate overthrow. But the Lord blasted and confounded all his designs; and his own life was taken away by the hand of an assassin.

Herod, arrayed in costly robes, addressed the people, and received the servile flatteries of the multitude, who honored him as a god. And for this he was smitten by worms in his vitals, and died by the hand of the Lord.

Some wicked men have been punished in the same manner and to the same extent as they have punished others.

Adonibezek, King of Bezek, though a great and successful warrior, was finally conquered. He fled before the army of Judah, but was pursued, caught and disabled by the cutting off of his thumbs and great toes. He acknowledged the justice of God in his punishment. "And Adonibezek said: 'Three score and ten Kings, having their thumbs and their great toes cut off, gathered their meat under my table. As I have done to them, so the Lord has requitted me.'"

Haman plotted the death of Mordecai, and erected for him a gallows fifty cubits high. But before the time of execution the King is undeceived, the cruel plot is discovered, and Haman is hung upon the gallows which he built for Mordecai.

A wicked son, enraged against his father, seized him by the hair of his head to drag him over the floor into the street. Having dragged him to the doorway, the miserable parent cried out: "Stop! Drag me no farther, for it was to this very spot that I dragged my father by the hair of his head."

CHAPTER X.

The Providence of God is seen in His interposition in behalf of nations.

How remarkably did God interpose in behalf of the Jewish nation.

How suitable was the person raised up to be their deliverer. How numerous and fearful were the plagues which were inflicted upon Pharaoh and the Egyptians till he let the people go. And how strange was the direction which he gave to the captive Jews when leaving the house of bondage. They might have taken a more direct course, and crossed over the Isthmus of Suez; but if they had done so they would have been overtaken and destroyed by the pursuing army. But God directed them to take a circuitous route and cross over at the Red Sea, which, as soon as reached, was opened before them. They crossed in safety; but the Egyptians, attempting to follow them, were drowned. The waters closed in upon them and all were lost. While the Red Sea was the pathway for His people, it was the grave of their enemies.

He was their guide, protector and kind benefactor all through their journey in the wilderness. He fought their battles, fed them with manna from heaven, giving them a double supply the day previous to the Sabbath, that there might be no gathering on the seventh day, thus teaching them to reverence and sanctify that holy day. He drew for them water from the flinty rock; led them by a pillar of cloud through the day, and by a flaming fire through the night. He interposed for them again when on the banks of the River Jordan. Here again the waters divided. Those above stood on heaps, while those below ran off into the Dead Sea. The priests who bore the Ark of the Covenant stood in the midst of the channel till all were safely landed on the opposite shore.

As they enter the Promised Land the walls of Jericho fall to the ground and crumble in ruins at the sound of the rams' horns and the shouts of the invading multitude.

He provided and prepared for them the Land of Promise. Wells which they never digged, houses which they never built, vineyards which they never planted, and lands which they had never cultivated were taken from the heathen—seven great and mighty nations—and given to them for their inheritance.

And all the calamities which afterwards befell them were His chastisements for their ingratitude and crimes.

The British nation has long been the object of God's kind, watchful care. Because she is, and has long been, an eminently

Christian nation, He has ever watched kindly over her.

She has long stood proudly among surrounding powerful nations. Rich in wealth, strong in power, and blessed with numerous Christian institutions, which are supported by a princely revenue, she occupies a lofty stand, and from her elevated station streams of light and glory are conveyed to distant lands.

She was the envy of the first Napoleon, who tried in vain to subdue her. The Spanish nation tried to enter and take possession of the little island, but to no purpose. Witness the failure of the Spanish armada. "The Papal Powers of Europe had resolved to reduce the British nation to her former condition of slavery and Popish darkness. They envied and detested her religion, her independence and her glory. They built and collected a formidable navy, the mightiest, perhaps, that had ever sailed on the seas. Assembled princes and Cardinals christened it the "Invincible Armada," and saw it set sail for the overthrow of Britain with no little ecstasy. But the very winds and waves that came from the shores of Britain seem to have caught the contagion of the island from which they came, and to set themselves in array against the advancing armament. Heaven and earth aided the apparently insignificant navy of Britain in the battle, for a mere wreck of the Spanish fleet returned to the shores of the Peninsula to proclaim, 'Not by power nor by might;'

and the British navy, victorious, and almost uninjured, returned to its native nursery of religion and piety, to impress yet more deeply the lesson we are most reluctant to learn: 'But by my spirit, saith the Lord.'"

The United States of America is another nation for which God has remarkably interposed. She occupies a large portion of a continent which God had mercifully kept undiscovered till needed by those who wished to flee from the oppressive and overgrown nations of Europe.

Ever since she has been a nation God has made her the object of His care and kind regard. He has fought her battles, freed her from the foul blot of slavery, blessed her with unparalleled prosperity, added millions to her population, made her great in arts and arms, the birthplace of science and the asylum of liberty. Her territory is immense, and her population is increasing on a scale more vast than ever before. And though she is flooded with Mormonism from the East, Romanism from Ireland, Materialism from Germany, Infidelity from France and Heathenism from China, yet her patriotism and her Christianity are rising above them all, and are making her the wonder and the admiration of the world.

How remarkably has God recently interposed in behalf of the people of Italy. Though once among the darkest, the most debased and enslaved of the Popish nations, through Divine interposition she has become a well organized and powerful kingdom ; has taken away the temporal power of the Pope, renounced the dogma of infalibility, proclaimed religious freedom, and made the city of Rome the Italian capital. "This is the Lord's doing, and it is marvelous in our eyes."

How severely and justly has God punished infidel France.

Voltaire and his associates in crime made their boast that they would soon overturn the foundations of the Christian religion, put a stop to the progress of the Gospel, and destroy the hope and consolation of godly men. And to what an alarming extent did they succeed. Then Christianity was renounced, the Christian Sabbath was abolished, Christian temples were deserted and desecrated, the Gospel was regarded as priestcraft, Christian ministers were represented as designing knaves, a vile prostitute was exhibited as the goddess of reason, and their country was drenched in blood. That was the fruit of her infidelity then.

And what is her condition now? The Communists who had recently the possession of Paris are no better than Voltaire and his guilty associates. To destroy all proper authority, to equalize the wealth of the nation, to shut up every Christian temple, to put a stop to all public worship, to cut asunder the marriage tie, and to live a life of licentiousness, are the principles which they held, and taught, and wished to become national. Her chastisements, then, though severe, are just. "For the nation and kingdom that will not serve Thee shall perish; yea, those nations shall be utterly wasted."

CHAPTER XI.

We have many remarkable interpositions of Providence in behalf of individuals for the accomplishment of His wise designs.

Look at God's servant, Job. In the early part of his life he ranked among the most distinguished men of the East. He was not only a patriarch, but a Judge and a Prince. His possessions were large; he was rich in flocks and herds, and his family was numerous and flourishing. The number of his flocks and herds is distinctly specified.

His substance was seven thousand sheep, three thousand camels, five hundred yoke of oxen, and five hundred she asses. Thus did "the Lord bless the work of his hands, and his substance was increased in the land."

The public estimation in which he was held is also specified. "When I went out to the gate through the city, when I prepared my seat in the street, the young men saw me and hid themselves, and the aged arose and stood up; the princes remained silent, and laid their hands on their mouths; the nobles held their peace and their tongues cleaved to the roofs of their mouths; when the ear heard me then it blessed me; when the eye saw me it gave witness for me, because I delivered the poor that cried, and the fatherless, and him that had none to help him. The blessing of him that was ready to perish came upon me; and I caused the widow's heart to sing for joy."

Yet it pleased God to visit this holy man with the most painful reverses of fortune. One messenger came close upon the heels of another with the sad tidings of calamity, distress and woe. One messenger came and told him that the Sabeans had taken his oxen and his asses and killed his servants with the sword. Another messenger came and told him that fire had fallen from heaven and had burned up his sheep and servants. A third came to tell him that the Chaldeans had taken away his camels and destroyed his servants. But the fourth came with still sadder tidings—this one came to tell him that a strong wind from the wilderness had blown down the house and killed all his sons and daughters. In the midst of these fearful calamities professed friends gathered around him for the avowed purpose of yielding him support and comfort. But from a harsh and ill-founded construction of the intention of Providence in these afflictions, they only aggravated his sorrows and increased his sufferings by their unjust and uncharitable upbraidings.

And did all this come by chance? Job thought very differently. He saw and acknowledged the hand of God in all the troubles through which he was called to pass. It was Job who said: "He holdeth back the face of His throne, and spreadeth His cloud upon it." And now, mark his conduct under his numerous and diversified sufferings. When required to curse God and die, he held fast his integrity. When urged to reproach his Maker, he vindicated his dealings. When death entered his family, and he was broken with breach upon breach, he bowed submissively and said: "The Lord gave and the Lord hath taken away; blessed be the name of the Lord." When robbed of his property, and left to stand on the ruins of his worldly hopes, he said: "Shall I receive good at the hand of the Lord, and shall I not receive evil?" "Though Thou slay me, yet will I put my trust in Thee." When his character was assailed by the tongue of calumny and the breath of slander, he said to his revilers:

"Have pity on me, have pity on me, O ye, my friends, for the hand of the Lord hath touched me." When looking forward to the day when secrets would be revealed, mysteries unraveled, and the drama of Providence wound up, how clearly and confidently does he speak of Christ and of his interest in Him: "I know that my Redeemer liveth, and that He shall stand upon the earth in the latter day, and though after my skin worms destroy this body, yet in my flesh shall I see God, whom I shall see for myself, and mine eyes shall behold and not another, though my reins be consumed within me."

I know there are those who doubt whether there ever was such a person as Job, and the inspiration of the book which bears his name, but none who respect and reverance the Bible can have any such doubts. The sacred penmen repeatedly refer both to the person and the book, as a divinely inspired record. Ezekiel refers to Job, places him by the side of Noah and Daniel, and speaks of him as a man of eminent piety. James says: "Ye have heard of the patience of Job, and have seen the end of the Lord; that the Lord is very pitiful and of tender mercy." Paul gives a quotation from the Book of Job: "For it is written, He taketh the wise in their own craftiness."

The purpose for which this book was written was to furnish an illustrious example of patience under the most intense trials and sufferings; and to show that true religion will bear the test of trial, even the severest to which it can be subjected.

See this exemplified in the case of Moses. A little rush bark is seen floating over the River Nile. It attracts the attention of Pharaoh's daughter. She opens the ark and finds in it a lovely babe. He meets with favor, and secures her affection. He is brought to her father's palace and to the Egyptian court. His mind is cultivated by education. He is schooled in all the learning of the country, and is eminently qualified to be a national legislator and military leader. And was all this done by chance? No; the hand of God was in the whole of it. He ordered every circumstance connected with that little bark. He it was that suggested the plan to the weeping mother, and then directed the steps of Pharaoh's daughter to the spot where the young child lay, excited her sympathy, and kindled in her heart a flame of love for the infant stranger. He watched over that little bark and its precious contents with constant care. Such was the mysterious plan which God devised to preserve and qualify Moses to be the leader, governor and defender of His people.

See the same truth also exemplified in the case of Joseph. A young shepherd boy dreams a dream which is interpreted of his future greatness. He is, on this account, hated by his brethren, is sold to the Ishmaelites, and carried into Egypt. There he is sold for a slave, is unjustly charged with crime and cast into prison; and there he becomes the interpreter of the dreams of the imprisoned butler and baker. This is carried to the ears of the King, who is greatly troubled on account of a dream. The distressed and injured youth is sent for, he makes known its interpretation, is on this account raised to power and placed on the highest pinacle of honor in the gift of the King. And did all this come by chance? No; it was all the contrivance of infinite wisdom. His evil disposed brethren who sold him, the Ishmaelites who carried him into Egypt, the licentious wife of Potipher, who wished to draw him into sin, and his master who cast him into prison, all these were only the sinful executioners of the Divine purpose. Joseph was sold into Egypt not only to provide bread for his family and posterity, but for the advancement of the Church.

In the whole of this mysterious providence God has one great object in view, and on this his eye is constantly and steadily fixed; it is the advancement of His glory in the salvation and happiness of His people.

We have another illustration of this truth in the case of Esther, the Queen of Ahasuerus. A little girl, a member of an obscure family in the land of Persia, is at an early age deprived, by the hand of death, of both her parents, and is left a poor orphan in the midst of a cold, unfeeling world. But as she advances in life she is virtuous, modest, beautiful, lovely and attractive.

The beautiful and amiable Esther attracts the attention and secures the affection of King Ahasuerus. She became his wife, was taken to his palace, and called to share the honors of his crown. And was all this mere accident? Were all these events brought about by chance? Certainly not. They were all the arrangements of infinite wisdom. By birth she belonged to the Jewish nation. Her people were scattered, surrounded by enemies, and plots were laid for their destruction. But in the palace of Sushan, and in the court of the King, Esther is true to her God, and true to her people, and her powerful influence is exerted for their protection and advancement. Thus was this poor, obscure girl raised up and guided by the hand of God to an elevated station and commanding influence, to be the protector and deliverer of His people; to prepare the way for their return to their native land, and to the Holy Hill of Zion.

We have another illustration of this truth in the case of Daniel.

The King of Babylon went to war with the King of Judah, is victorious in battle, and among the captives taken away from their homes and country is a pious and amiable youth belonging to one of the royal families of the Jews. He is taken into the family of the King of Babylon. He stands before the King. He is daily fed at his table. He receives the royal favor, is advanced to power, and stands upon one of the highest pinacles of honor. In this elevated station he is not only true to his King, but true to the God of his fathers. In this situation he became an object of envy. A wicked plot was laid for his downfall and ruin, and he is threatened with the lions' den if he prays to any God but Nebuchadnezzar's senseless image. But the youthful saint is no idolater; he can worship no god but the Lord God of Israel. Having been found praying, as usual, to the God of his Fathers, he was cast into a den of lions. But in this perilous situation his God was with him who laid the ferocious lions at his feet, like so many harmless lambs. And was all this mere accident? Certainly not. His enemies designed it for evil; but God designed it for good. Thus the Divine purpose was accomplished, Daniel was saved, idolatry was renounced, and the God of Israel was publicly honored, and universally worshipped.

And what a striking illustration have we of this truth in the case of the three young Hebrews. These young men, like Daniel, were of the royal family of Judah, and with him were carried captive into Babylon.

For three years they were brought up in the King's palace; fed at the King's table, and instructed in all the learning of the Chaldeans. And such was the proficiency which they made, and their growing uprightness and integrity, that they were soon elevated to some of the most honorable and lucrative situations in the kingdom. On this account they were the objects of envy and malice, and a plot was laid for their downfall and ruin. They were required to fall down and worship a senseless image, and were threatened with a fearful death should they dare to refuse. But they did nobly refuse. The threatening of death—and death in its most terrific form—could not move them to a sinful compliance; and when told that if they persevered in their determination they would be cast into a burning, fiery furnace, their resolution was unshaken; they evinced a spirit of noble daring. With dignified composure and believing confidence, they said: "O, King Nebuchadnezzar, we are not careful to answer thee in this matter. If it be so, the God whom we serve is able to deliver us from the burning, fiery furnace, and

He will deliver us out of thy hand, O, King. But if not, supposing He should not interpose in our behalf, and we should be cast into the flames, and perish in the flames, whatever may befall us, be it known unto thee, O, King, that we will not serve thy gods nor worship the graven image which thou hast set up." To punish them for this act of disobedience, amid the cries and shrieks of friends, and the insolent triumph of foes, they were cast into the furnace heated seven times hotter than it was wont to be heated, by the orders of an enraged and merciless tyrant. But in that furnace, and in the midst of those flames, there was immediately with them a fourth like unto the son of man, and by him they were preserved and cheered. They were cast into the flames, but in those flames they remained unhurt. Not a single hair of their heads was singed; nor did the least smell of fire pass upon their garments. The bands by which they were bound were loosened and they walked at liberty in the midst of the flames. And how is this to be accounted for? The Omnipotent Redeemer was with them, His power protected them, and His grace was abundantly sufficient for them.

But let us now come nearer to our own times to see this truth illustrated.

During the dark days of Popery, Tyndal's Bible sold with great difficulty, and had nearly ruined those who engaged in the enterprise, when the Popish Bishop of London, to stay the progress of truth, bought up an immense number of copies to burn them, which freed its publishers from debt, and they were enabled to print and circulate a second and much larger edition. Thus an immense amount of good was accomplished by an interposition of Providence in overruling this wicked act of the Bishop, for the advancement of His truth.

During the days of Mary, the Popish and cruel Queen of England, a person was sent with an edict for destroying the Protestants of Ireland. In the city of Chester, while lodging in the house of the Mayor, he happened to mention the nature of his commission. A woman who overheard him make this statement abstracted this cruel edict from his possession. When, therefore, he arrived before the authorities of Ireland his commission was missing. He had to go back to London to obtain a second, but before his return to Ireland the Queen died. Thus did God mercifully interfere to save the Protestants of Ireland from an untimely and cruel death.

Lady Huntington was a devoted, active Christian. She lived for the good of others, and the advancement of the Saviour's kingdom. She spent a large income in the support of charitable and religious objects. And sometimes she went beyond her means, and involved herself in pecuniary difficulties. At such times she was accustomed to lift up her heart to God, in all the confidence of faith, and call on Him for help.

I will give one instance of God's interposition in her behalf: "Zion Chapel, near White Chapel, London, which was formerly a riding-school, was offered for sale, and was taken by the Countess of Huntington, at a venture, in hope of benefitting the depraved and crowded population of that district. But, though her ladyship bought it, she had not funds to pay for it. Five hundred pounds had to be paid down by a certain day. A gentleman who called upon her about noon of the same day that payment was to be made, asked her if she had received the expected sum. She wept, and replied that she had not; 'but,' said her ladyship, 'I have been greatly comforted by thinking of those lines by Sternhold and Hopkins:

" Make you His service your delight ;
He'll make your wants His care." '

The gentleman blamed her ladyship greatly for engaging in such strange speculations. While he was yet speaking, the post came in and brought three letters ; and when she opened and read the third she wept. The gentleman inquired into the cause of her tears. 'There,' said she, 'take that letter and see. " O, thou of little faith, wherefore didst thou doubt ?" ' repeating again the lines of Sternhold and Hopkins. The gentleman took the letter and read as follows : ' A gentleman having heard of the efforts of the Countess of Huntington to promote the Gospel about the metropolis, sends her five hundred pounds.' " And was all this mere accident ? Did all come by chance ? Certainly not. It was a kind interposition of Providence. Here was the exact sum needed, sent by a stranger for the object for which it was required, and on the day when payment had to be made.

The mistake of a word in the direction of a letter led to the discovery of the gunpowder plot, by which means the life of the British King and the members of Parliament were saved from a fearful and cruel death. And was this mere accident? No; it was a merciful interposition of Providence. It was the finger of God pointing out the diabolical plot.

The American Continent is provided, and kept in reserve, to furnish room and support for the overgrown nations of Europe. As soon as it is needed, Columbus is ready and anxious to go in search of it. His sovereign and the government of his country favor the enterprise. All things necessary for the voyage are readily furnished, and the enterprising explorer sets sail with high hopes and ardent desires. But at length the disappointed crew get discouraged, become mutinous, and resolve to throw Columbus, their brave commander, overboard. But at this juncture a straggling sea weed floats in full view before them, to indicate their near approach to land. Hope is again revived, the mariners are cheered, the life of Columbus is saved, and the Continent is discovered. And did all this come by chance? No; all was under the management of a superintending Providence. And for this rich inheritance generations yet unborn will thank Him with warm emotions of grateful hearts.

CHAPTER XII.

The Providence of God is seen in making all things work together for the ultimate good of His Church.

God has a perfect knowledge of all His people. Not a single member of His Church, however obscure, can escape His notice, or be deprived of His watchful care. He has a Book of Life in which their names are written, and a book of remembrance in which all their pious deeds and labors of love are recorded. "For the eyes of the

Lord run to and fro throughout the whole earth, to show himself strong in behalf of them whose hearts are perfect toward Him."

The course of nature has been controlled for the good of the Church. I do not recollect, in the whole of Sacred History, that we have a single instance of God going out of the common line of His providential dealings but where His people, in one way or other, have been connected. As, by reason of sin, nature was armed against man, so, on his return to God, contrary to her own laws, she is made subservient to his security and salvation. Hence, we see the sea divide for His people to pass through dry shod. For them the stars are marshaled to fight against Sisera. For them the sun stands still upon

Gibeon, and the moon in the Valley of Ajalon. He cast down upon the enemies of His people great hail stones, "so that more were they who fell by the hail stones than Israel slew by the sword." For them the fire loses its burning quality; and ferocious lions lie at their feet like harmless lambs.

The affairs of nations have been controlled by a kind Providence for the good of the Church.

By reason of the judgments which God brought upon the Egyptians, He made it more their interest to let the people go than to retain them in bondage. Sometimes He raises up Kings for the express purpose of vindicating the rights of His people, and avenging their wrongs. "Therefore," said the prophet Elisha to Jehu, "I have anointed thee king over the people of the Lord that I may avenge the blood of my servants, the prophets, and the blood of all the servants of the Lord at the hand of Jezebel." He also raised up Cyrus to deliver the visible Church from Babylon, at the expiration of their seventy years' captivity. He also caused that people, contrary to all rules of civil policy, not only to deliver them, and restore them to their own land, but to assist them in rebuilding their city and temple. Thus we see that "the hearts of all men are in His hands, and He turneth them what way soever He pleaseth."

The gifts and talents of men, in every age of the world, by a wise arrangement of Provi-

dence, have been used for the good of the Church.

That unseen hand which rules the destinies of nations, in an especial manner rules in Zion; and the wisdom of His government most eminently appears in adapting both the talents and the graces of His servants to the age in which they live, the people over whom they preside, and the work to which they are called.

Who but Noah, in the midst of reproach, ridicule and the most discouraging prospects of success, would have persevered in the discharge of his duties for the space of a hundred and twenty years.

Who but Moses was qualified for such an undertaking as that to which he was appointed? Who else could have surmounted the difficulties which he had to surmount, and to bear the insults and reproaches which he had to meet from that ungrateful and provoking people?

Who but the Apostle Paul could have labored so incessantly, endured reproaches and persecutions, bonds and imprisonments, and have planted the Gospel in so many nations, so different in their customs, manners and habits?

Who but Luther, who, aided by the eternal spirit, resolved to do battle with demons, and to hurl disgrace against the Pope, could have brought about so extensive and glorious a reformation as that which followed his labors and immortalized his name?

Who but Whitfield and Wesley were qualified for the great work to which they were appointed? They lived and labored at a time when vital piety was almost extinct, when the masses of the nation were irreligious and immoral, and were led captive by the devil at his will. But through their zealous, self-denying labors, and faithful, earnest exhibitions of Divine truth tens of thousands became the subjects of conscious guilt and Gospel salvation.

These were all men for the times, raised up by God for the good of the Church.

In every age the Lord has had His morning stars in the Church, as heavenly luminaries, to shed abroad a savor of the knowledge of a crucified Redeemer.

Angels are appointed by a superintending Providence to act for the good of the Church. Hence, they are called watchers, messengers, and ministers, sent forth to minister to those who shall be heirs of salvation. Sometimes a whole company of angels have been engaged for a single servant of God. When Jacob went to meet his brother Esau he was sore afraid; but the Lord sent a whole company of angels to defend him from the wrath of his brother. Therefore, it is said: "Jacob went on his way, and the angels of God met him, and when he saw them he said: 'This is the Lord's host.'"

Time would fail me to advert to the numerous instances recorded in the Holy Scriptures of the kind offices which these invisible attendants have performed for the people of God. But this we can with truth say: that the weakest and the meanest of God's servants are more highly honored by the attendance of these unseen legions than all the greatest potentates upon earth, with all their legions of honor about them.

Those things which in themselves have a tendency to create strife and contention are overruled by a kind Providence for the good of the Church.

Divisions in the Church have been overruled for her good. The separation of Paul and Barnabas, which was occasioned by a painful contention, was for the Church's enlargement. One denomination has been divided into many others, and yet the parent body is larger than ever.

The diversity of opinion which prevails in the Church with regard to doctrine, discipline and government, which short-sighted men have employed as a weapon against her, has been overruled by Providence for her enlargement and prosperity. Was it not for diversity of sentiment, the Church would be like a stagnated pool. In proof of this, take a view of those countries where free inquiry in matters of religion is not tolerated. There you see the people sunk down, and lost in all the rubbish of superstition and idolatry. Free inquiry in matters of religion is the birthright of every man. Every man has a right to think for himself, to form his own creed, and to worship God as his own conscience may dictate. And no man, nor any number of men, have any right to force their creed upon him.

Diversity of sentiment among Christian believers excites emulation, enkindles zeal, leads to investigation, and stimulates to exertion.

Persecution itself, which has often been employed to exterminate the Church, has uniformly, by a kind, watchful Providence, been made the means of her extension.

The persecution which arose at the death of Stephen, though it scattered the Church, yet it was like the husbandman that scatters abroad the precious seed which produces an abundant crop, for wherever these persecuted saints went they scattered abroad the seeds of the kingdom, by which means the Church was greatly enlarged.

It is to the persecutions that befell the Apostle Paul that the Church is indebted for many of those invaluable epistles which he wrote. And it is to persecution that we are indebted for many of the best books that are now extant in the English languge.

Christ was given for the good of the Church. This is the greatest and the richest display of Providence, around which almost all other providences are seen to merge. To this we trace the calling of Abraham, the institution of the Livitical ritual, all that Moses in the law and the prophets wrote, and the management by which the Jews were kept a separate and distinct people, not only separate and distinct from other nations, but among themselves, so that every one knew his own tribe, and the patriarch from which he descended.

The Church is the purchase of the Saviour's passion, the subject of His meditation, and will be His joy and crown of rejoicing, "when He shall see of the travel of His soul, and shall be satisfied."

He is the head of His mystical body. He is the King of Zion, and overrules all things for the good of His Church.

It cannot be otherwise that all God's providential arrangements are for the good of His Church, *because of the great love which He has ever manifested toward her.*

Such is His love for the Church that she is said to be engraven on the palms of His hands, in allusion to the rings where men engrave the likeness of those dear to them; and as the Jews engraved on their rings the likeness of their city during their captivity, that they might never forget it. The love of God for His Church is greater, far greater, than that felt by a tender-hearted mother for her infant child. And can He so love His Church and not plan and govern for her good? No; she is ever the object of His care.

Such is the love which God feels for His Church that He favors those who favor her; and He is the enemy of all those who despise and persecute her.

Moab gave entertainment to the flying Israelites when their land was invaded by an enemy, and for that favor the Lord said that the spoiler should not enter their territories; and that He would give them kings and judges under the protection of the house of David. But observe, on the other hand, the fearful curse which God pronounced upon those who came not out to meet the Israelites with bread and water. They were not allowed to enter the congregation of His people for ten generations.

God has more love for one righteous person than for a whole city of the ungodly. He would not suffer a spark of fire, or a drop of brimstone to fall upon the cities of the plain, till His servant Lot was safe in Zoar. God has more love for one righteous person than for a whole world of sinners. He saves Noah, and his family on his account; but He drowns an ungodly world. And we are assured that if only ten righteous persons had been found in the cities of Sodam and Gomorrah God would have spared them for their sakes.

And why are Christian nations spared and defended, while others are distracted and tumble into ruins? Shall we attribute it to their wise politicians, to their able statesmen, to their brave generals, to their numerous armies, or to their powerful navies? No; none of these; nor all of them put together; but to God's watchful care over His Church, listening to the prayers of His saints, who sigh and cry for the abominations of the world.

CHAPTER XIII.

The inferences which are to be drawn from the preceding interpositions of Providence :—

If all the providences are for the good of the Church, *then we may fairly infer that God has a Church in the world*—a people for His glory. A people separated from the world, the subjects of His grace, who voluntarily associate together for Christian fellowship and religious worship, and over whom He exercises a constant watchful care.

If there is a constant watchful Providence over the Church, *then we may justly infer that He always will have a Church in the world.* She can never be destroyed. Thundering anathemas have been poured out against her. Infidels, by craft, and tyrants, by power, have invented for her modes of torture and of death. Her enemies have been assaulting her for the space of six thousand years; but every past assault has gone to prove her stability, while every future assault shall be had in derision by Him who sitteth in the heavens. But after all that her enemies have done she still lives and is still enlarging her borders. The King of Zion is going on from conquering unto conquest, "and will reign till all enemies are put under His feet." "On this rock will I build my Church, and the gates of hell shall not prevail against her."

If God will always have a Church in the world, *then we may infer again that He will always provide for her wants.* She will never be without a regular succession of devoted members, wise and zealous officers, faithful and successful ministers. If Abel be put to death, God will raise up a Seth to fill his place. If Nebuchadnezzar be permitted to pull down the walls of Jerusalem, a Cyrus will be raised to build them up again. So it will ever be in the Christian ministry. These faithful, devoted servants of God are almost daily taken from the Church and carried by fiery chariots to heaven. Some are taken away newly green, others newly gray, while a few are allowed to drop their flowing mantles at the age of three score years and ten. But no sooner has this fiery car dislodged one than another steps forward and says: "Here am I. Lord, send me."

If God has a Church in this world, *then we may infer again that it is the duty of every member to study her welfare.* Then let every member promote her peace, pray for her prosperity, labor for her advancement, and emulate the example of the pious Jew, who, in the strength of his attachment, and from the fullness of his heart, said: "If I forget thee, O, Jerusalem, let my right hand forget her cunning; if I do not remember thee, let my tongue cleave to the roof of my mouth, if I prefer not Jerusalem above my chief joy."

CHAPTER XIV.

The answers which are given to the objectors of God's providential interpositions:

The objectors to God's providential interpositions ask, if there be a watchful providence continually presiding over the children of men, how can this be reconciled with the unequal distributions of His blessings? How is it, they ask, that the wicked are often treated as friends and the righteous as enemies? The wicked, they say, are often blessed with prosperity, and the righteous are sometimes reduced to poverty and want. We have seen, they say, the wicked rioting in luxury, and swiming in splendor, while the righteous have been reproached and persecuted, and sometimes dragged before an impious magistrate, or a blood-thirsty tyrant; or, like a poor Lazarus, lie neglected and unpitied at the gate of an imperious and merciless lord. I admit the correctness of the contrast, but not the inference. The day is approaching when the secret will be revealed, when the mystery will be unraveled, when the great drama of providence will be wound up, and will appear before assembled worlds that all the ways of God to men are just and equal.

But we contend that it is not *well* with

the wicked in prosperity, nor *ill* with the righteous in adversity.

Can it be *well* with those who are bartering immortal pleasures for momentary gratifications? Can it be *well* with those who, instead of being better, are the worse for the blessings bestowed and favors conferred upon them? They may be rich in the estimation of the world, but in the estimation of heaven, "they are poor and blind, miserable and naked." They may be elevated to pinacles of honor and dignity among men, but in the estimation of heaven they are sunk down into the low depths of sin and depravity. They may put on a cheerful countenance and appear gay and happy, when the heart is full of bitterness, and the mind is as the troubled sea when it cannot rest. The wicked have now their good things, but it is all the good they will ever enjoy.

As it is not *well* with the wicked in prosperity, so it is not *ill* with the righteous in adversity. Adversity cannot be a positive evil, nor can prosperity be a positive good. A bad man may be miserable in prosperity, and a good man may be happy in adversity. Can it then be *ill* with those whose guilt is canceled, whose hearts are changed, and who are filled with peace and joy through believing? Can it be *ill* with those to whom God is a reconciled Father, Christ is a Saviour, and the Holy Ghost is a comforter? I ask again, can it be *ill* with those who are suffering only momentary pains for immortal pleasures? "who can stand and rejoice in hope of the glory of God;" and who can anticipate by faith the happy day when the calamities of time will be exchanged for the glories of eternity? No; it is *well* with the righteous in every situation and condition in which they can be placed. "Godliness with contentment is great gain." "Godliness is profitable unto all things having the promise of the life that now is and of that which is to come."

But the great good of the righteous *is in reversion*—it is laid up for them. Shame will be made the pathway to glory, and death the way to immortality and eternal life. Then a poor Lazarus will be comforted, while his rich, unfeeling lord will be tormented.

If good men are poor, tired and afflicted, it is always for some wise end; to answer some valuable purpose, which, if we know not now, we shall know hereafter. Let us then confide in a kind Providence, who makes all things work together for our present and future good.

CONCLUSION.

Trust Providence in the greatest extremity. In the day of adversity, in the hour of persecution, in the time of sickness, on the ruins of your worldly hopes, at the grave of your dearest earthly object, and on a bed of death, trust Him who has pledged His gracious presence and comforting support. Take Him at His word. He has pledged, and His pledge has never been broken, and consequently the soul of the confiding Christian has never been deserted.

Trust Providence in the use of means. Let there be a full consecration of yourselves to His service, a diligent improvement of your privileges, a constant employment of your talents for the advancement of the Saviour's kingdom; and in the full assurance of faith, let your heart be lifted up to God in earnest prayer, if you would witness His kind interposition in your behalf.

Let the consideration of a kind, watchful Providence promote your religious advancement. Let it strengthen your faith, inflame your love, embolden you in prayer, encourage you in difficulties, correct and modify your anxiety about the future events of life, and induce you to leave all your affairs in the hands of the wise Ruler of the universe.

Let the Christian console himself with the assurance that the darkest dispensations of providence are limited by time. While upon earth his graces will be tried by a variety of sorrows and complicated distresses. It is only when he breathes his last that the effects of the curse will cease to follow him. It is only when he steps into the deep, cold flood to cross the river of death that his troubles will come to an end. It is only in the paradise of God above that he will enjoy uninterrupted and eternal repose. Then he will be delivered from all his tribulations, for they can only follow him to the grave.

But while the sorrows of the confiding Christian are limited by time, his prospects of future happiness are boundless as eternity.

Then he will enter a kingdom that wlll never be moved; he will wear a crown that will never tarnish, and possess an inheritance that fadeth not away. Then his day will never be followed by night. His light will never be eclipsed or overspread by darkness. His joy will never be succeeded by sorrow. He will enjoy a nightless day; a perpetual Sabbath—a deathless immortality. Such are the cheering prospects of the Christian as he steps from the shores of time into the boundless ocean of immortal glory and endless blessedness.

We have a comprehensive and beautiful illustration of God's providential dealings and their beneficial results, by Cowper, in the following admirable lines:

" God moves in a mysterious way
His wonders to perform ;
He plants His footsteps in the sea,
And rides upon the storm.

" Deep in unfathomable mines
Of never-failing skill,
He treasures up His bright designs,
And works His sovereign will.

" Ye fearful saints, fresh courage take ;
The clouds ye so much dread
Are big with mercy, and will break
In blessings on your head.

" Judge not the Lord by feeble sense,
But trust Him for His grace.
Behind a frowning Providence
He hides a smiling face.

" His purposes will ripen fast—
Unfolding every hour ;
The bud may have a bitter taste,
But sweet will be the flower.

" Blind unbelief is sure to err,
And scan His work in vain ;
God is His own interpreter,
And He will make it plain."

We will now close our vindication of a superintending Providence. He may lead us about. His footsteps may be in the sea. His chastisements may be severe. His way may be crooked as the paths of the desert, and dark as the hour of midnight, yet we have this delightful assurance: "The Judge of all the earth will do right." Let us, then, trust Him where we cannot trace Him.

www.ingramcontent.com/pod-product-compliance
Lightning Source LLC
LaVergne TN
LVHW021413110826
845150LV00007B/1913

* 9 7 8 1 4 2 5 5 1 0 6 3 3 *